BBC

ABOUT THE AUTHOR

The author developed an interest in home computing whilst working on microelectronic projects at the Microelectronics Applications Unit, U.M.I.S.T., where he held the position of Chief Electronics Technician. Still in the employ of U.M.I.S.T., he teaches BASIC programming at Whitefield Adult Education Centre, Greater Manchester. He is a member of the Society of Electronics and Radio Technicians and is a Licentiate of the City and Guilds of London Institute.

A Concise Introduction to the Language of BBC BASIC

by

T. J. E. Murphy

BERNARD BABANI (publishing) LTD
THE GRAMPIANS
SHEPHERDS BUSH ROAD
LONDON W6 7NF
ENGLAND

PLEASE NOTE

Although every care has been taken with the production of this book to ensure that any projects, designs, modifications and/or programs etc. contained herein, operate in a corrrect and safe manner and also that any components specified are normally available in Great Britain, the Publishers do not accept responsibility in any way for the failure, including fault in design, of any project, design, modification or program to work correctly or to cause damage to any other equipment that it may be connected to or used in conjunction with, or in respect of any other damage or injury that may be so caused, nor do the Publishers accept responsibility in any way for the failure to obtain specified components.

Notice is also given that if equipment that is still under warranty is modified in any way or used or connected with home-built equipment then that warranty may be void.

First Published – May 1985

British Library Cataloguing in Publication Data
Murphy, T. J. E.
A concise introduction to the language of
BBC BASIC. – (BP149)
1. BBC Microcomputer – Programming
2. Electron (Computer) – Programming
3. Basic (Computer program language)
I. Title
001.64'24 QA76.8.E./

ISBN 0 85934 124 0

Printed and Bound in Great Britain by Cox & Wyman Ltd, Reading

I should like to thank
Jeff Bradbury and my wife Ita,
for their help and assistance in
the preparation of this book.

Preface

The past two years has seen an avalanche of microcomputers in the domestic environment made possible with the availability of inexpensive integrated circuits, namely, CPUs and RAM and ROM devices. However, probably the greatest impact has been made with the introduction of microcomputers in schools. With government support, most schools in the U.K. have at least one microcomputer system and with Computer Studies available at O and A Level, a computer-literate society is in the making. The BBC Microcomputer has played a major role and is to be found in most schools, universities and other educational establishments.

The BBC Microcomputer, from a hardware point of view together with the facilities it offers, represents excellent value for money but perhaps its most attractive feature is its dialect of BASIC. The features offered by BBC BASIC provide the newcomer to computer programming with a simple and easy-to-learn, yet powerful and extremely well-structured version of BASIC, ideally suited to the beginner, student or enthusiast.

This small book is an attempt to provide a clear and concise short course on BBC BASIC, the text of which has been compiled from lecture notes written whilst teaching BASIC programming to adults at an Adult Education Centre.

This concise introduction to BBC BASIC should be read whilst using the BBC Microcomputer and its User Manual. All example programs should be typed in and run before progressing to the next topic – all programs have been reproduced from original hard copies in an attempt to eliminate program listing errors.

The contents closely follows the O Level syllabus for Computer Studies of the Joint Metriculation Board and may therefore prove useful to students preparing for the examination.

T.J.E.Murphy

Contents

Introduction

A computer is an electronic machine designed to process information. Computers can also calculate, store information, sort information, etc. They can be instructed to make decisions, but a computer cannot think for itself.

Information to be processed by a computer is called Data.

Incorrect data given to the computer will result in incorrect data out, hence the term: "Garbage in, garbage out".

A computer will act in response to instructions; without instructions it is useless. A set of instructions to a computer is called a Program. The computer can store a large number of instructions and then work through them one at a time.

A computer is indeed a data processing device and has three main stages:

(i) Input – Data supplied – Program;
(ii) Processor – Computes and controls;
(iii) Output – Results printed out.

It is very important to ensure that the input, i.e., data or program which the computer receives is, (a) accurate and, (b) given in logical sequence:

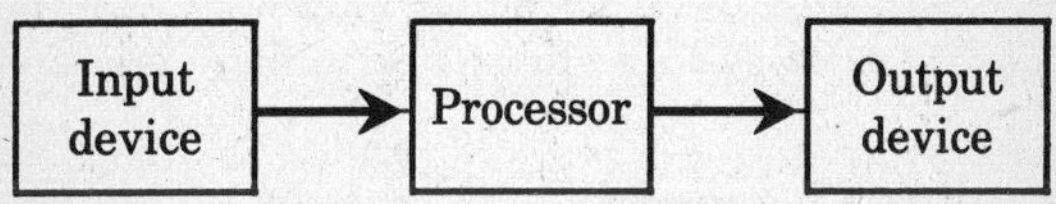

Computers can perform the above tasks at incredible speeds, performing millions of operations in a second. Vast amounts of information can be stored in its memory and it may have access to other huge memory banks. They do work of a highly repetitive nature; are consistent in giving results; are extremely accurate and are very reliable.

Computer Program

A computer program is a set of simple instructions which when carried out by a computer form a step-by-step solution to a given problem. The art of good programming is to break down a problem you wish to present to the computer into a precise enough form, i.e., expressed as a logical sequence of events.

BASIC

BASIC is an acronym for **B**eginner's **A**ll-purpose **S**ymbolic **I**nstruction **C**ode. It is simple in structure; has a small vocabulary and is used extensively for beginners to computing. BASIC is a high-level language, i.e., problem orientated and although simple to use, it is powerful enough to satisfy a wide range of applications. It is suited to the solution of mathematical problems and the processing of textual information. BASIC is probably the most commonly used computer language, albeit in many different versions and dialects.

Algorithm

An Algorithm is a logical sequence of events leading to the successful solution to a given problem. If a computer program is written and then RUN and it successfully solves the problem concerned, then the algorithm is said to be correct. Typical examples of everyday algorithms are: Cake Recipies, Knitting Patterns, Kit Assembly Instructions, etc.

Language Elements

BASIC is designed to handle numerical and alphabetical information (alphanumeric). Numbers are known as numeric constants and strings of characters forming text are known as string constants.

Numeric constants

Numeric constants can be in the form of Integers, i.e. whole numbers or Floating-point numbers, i.e. numbers with a decimal point and a fractional part, for example:

```
29,4,67
0.91,46.79
```

Negative numbers are preceded by a minus sign, and very large and very small floating-point numbers may be represented in an exponential form, i.e., a floating-point number (the mantissa) is followed by the letter "E" and an optionally signed integer (the exponent), for example:

```
235.988E-4  =  0.0235988
    2359E6  =  2359000000
```

The range of minimum to maximum integer numbers that can be processed by the BBC Microcomputer is −2147483648 to +2147483647.

String constants
A string constant is a string of characters (alphanumeric). Strings must start with a letter and the length of a string can be up to a maximum of 255 characters long, for example:

```
"hello"
"littlehampton 235"
```

NB: All strings must be enclosed in quotation marks. A space is regarded as a character.

Numeric variables
Variables are names used to identify memory locations (RAM) in a computer. A value may be assigned to a particular memory location, say, location "X" and this value can be changed at any time, for example:

Variable ↘ ↙ Constant

```
X  = 47.89
A1 = 15
G7 = 106
```

NB: Integer variables (whole numbers) use the per cent sign (%) as the declaration character, e.g., B%=47.

String variables
String variables are used to identify memory locations that contain strings of characters. A string variable always ends with a dollar sign ($), for example:

```
A$ = "hello"
X$ = "14th AUGUST 1983"
NAME$ = "GEORGE"
```

As a matter of interest, all keyboard characters are represented internally by the computer allocating each character with a numeric code known as the ASCII Code, e.g. "A" is given the unique value of 65 (lowest value), and "Z" has code value 90 (highest value). Therefore, when comparing strings, BASIC compares the corresponding number code of each string, e.g., if the string associated with X$ is "APPLE" and that with Y$ is "BALL", then the value of X$ is less than Y$ since the value of "A" is less than the value of "B". Thus, it can be seen that String Sorting in BASIC is quite a simple matter as indeed is Numeric Sorting.

NB: Whilst you can add, subtract, multiply and divide using numeric variables, the only mathematical function allowed using string variables is addition, for example:

```
10 A$ = "TUESDAY "
20 B$ = "MARCH 15th"
30 C$ = A$+B$
40 PRINT C$

RUN
```

RUN this program to find the result. Note the space after TUESDAY in line 10.

This is called Concatenation using +.

Operators

Operators are functions or procedures which affect one or more items when used, e.g., comparing one item with another. There are four groups:

(i) Arithmetic;
(ii) Relational;
(iii) Logical;
(iv) Functional.

(i) Arithmetic operators

Operator	*Operation*	*Example*
+	Addition	`PRINT 9+3`
−	Subtraction	`PRINT 6-4+3`
*	Multiplication	`PRINT 12*12`
/	Division	`PRINT 16/2`
^	Raise to the power	`PRINT 9^2`

NB: In BASIC there is an order of precedence when using arithmetic operators, i.e., everything within parentheses is evaluated first, then ^, $-x$ (negative numbers), *, /, + and −.

(ii) Relational operators

Operator	*Operation*	*Example*
=	Equal to	`X=Y`
<>	Not equal to	`X<>Y`
<	Less than	`X<Y`
>	Greater than	`X>Y`
<=	Less than or equal to	`X<=Y`
>=	Greater than or equal to	`X>=Y`

(iii) Logical operators
AND, OR, NOT, for example:

```
IF A=4 AND B=6 THEN.........
IF A<4 OR  B=25 THEN........
IF NOT (A=8 AND B=3) THEN...
```

(iv) Functional operators
A function is used in an expression to call a predetermined operation that is to be performed, for example:

`SQR` = Square root
`SIN` = Sine

```
COS = Cosine
TAN = Tangent
```

Program Structure

A BASIC program is made up of a series of simple instructions written as a set of BASIC statements. Each statement is written on a single line and each line starts off with its own line number.

Line numbers indicate to the computer the order in which the instructions are to be executed; lowest line number first – highest last. They indicate the logical sequence and facilitate program modification.

NB: The computer will continue to store lines of program in its memory until the program is complete and the computer is told to RUN it. However, instant action from the computer will result in the use of "command" words, for example:

```
PRINT"HELLO"
```

It is common practice when line numbering a computer program to allocate line numbers in increments of 10, i.e., 10, 20, 30, 40, 50, etc., since this allows useful space between instructions for modification and/or line additions.

NB: BBC BASIC provides the keyword AUTO for this purpose. If selected, it automatically provides line numbers when typing in a listing.

Line Format

Line number Statement <RETURN>

More than one BASIC statement may be placed on a line but each statement on a line must be separated from the last by a colon (:), for example:

Line number Statement : Statement <RETURN>

BASIC Keywords

A programming language is a vocabulary of keywords and symbols with a set of rules called Syntax (grammar).

The following is a list with descriptions and examples of words that BASIC understands. These words are called Keywords and most keywords in BASIC can be used as commands and as statements in a program. If used as a command word, immediate response from the computer is obtained but if contained in a statement, it only results in a screen print-out when the program is RUN.

PRINT

This is an output command and it tells the computer to print out the data onto the VDU or TV screen, for example:

(a) `PRINT"my first line"`

(b) `print"my first line"`

Line Numbers

Remark is used for comments you wish to make for your own use and for others using your program. This line is ignored by computer.

(c)
```
10 REM PRINT PROGRAM
20 PRINT"basic is easy"
30 PRINT
40 PRINT"when you know the rules"
50 END
```

All keywords must be in upper case lettering.

End of program.

Text after PRINT must always be enclosed in quotes.

NB: (a) is not a program line and results in immediate print-out on pressing <RETURN>;

(b) here "print" is in lower case and the computer does not recognise it as a keyword, therefore the computer indicates "MISTAKE".

REMEMBER (i) to press the <RETURN> key at the end of each program line. This indicates end of instruction and prompts the computer to put the program line into memory;

(ii) to type RUN on completion of typing in program. This initiates the execution of the program:

```
  5 REM PRINT AND PUNCTUATION
 10 LET X=5
 20 PRINT X,X*2,X/2
 30 PRINT
 40 PRINTX;X;X
 50 PRINT
 60 PRINTX'X
 70 PRINT
 80 PRINTTAB(20);X
 90 END
```

```
RUN
          5         10        2.5

          555

          5
          5

                    5
```

The "Print and Punctuation" program above introduces two new keywords, i.e., LET and TAB as well as demonstrating the use of punctuation when using PRINT.

Note that below the program are the tabulated results of the output obtained when the program is RUN.

NB: *Commas* force items to be printed in columns, ten characters wide;

Semi-colons force items to be printed next to each other on the same line;

Apostrophe will force print-out to a new line.

TAB

TAB can be used with PRINT to specify a print position of a character or alternatively, prints a certain number of spaces, e.g. as in line 80 above, where PRINTTAB(20);X prints out spaces ending at the 20th character position and then prints the value assigned to the variable X.

When two numbers are held within parentheses then the TAB statement will result in the character being printed on a screen co-ordinate, e.g., PRINTTAB(3,14);X will cause the value of X to appear on the screen 4 characters across and 15 lines down.

LET

LET is an assignment statement; it assigns a value to a variable, e.g., LET X=5, i.e. memory location X is given the value 5. This can be changed at any time. LET is optional – X=5 is acceptable and will work in a program.

LIST

This command tells the computer to list any program held in memory and print it out to a VDU screen and/or a Printer. It is most useful when debugging a program or during program modification. Individual lines may be listed or a selected group of lines as well as entire programs. Very long programs that scroll past may be stopped through by typing <CTRL> N (both keys simultaneously) and then listing. This allows one to examine a program page by page on pushing the <SHIFT> key. <CTRL> O will reset to scroll mode, for example:

```
 5 REM LIST PROGRAM
10 LET X=20
20 LET Y=5
30 LET Z=X-Y
40 PRINTX,Y,Z
50 END
```

Type in these commands and observe results:

```
LIST        – Lists entire program
LIST 1Ø,3Ø  – Lists lines 10 to 30
LIST 4Ø     – Lists line 40
```

At this point it may be wise to introduce two very useful keywords which will assist especially when typing in long program listings:

NEW

NEW clears all stored text so that a new piece of text can be typed in. It should always be typed in before entering a new program.

OLD

OLD is used to recover a program which has been cleared by NEW or by having pressed the <BREAK> key. Programs can only be recovered if no program lines have been entered.

NB: If it is necessary to stop or interrupt a program during running or entering in, use the <ESCAPE> key. This will provide a temporary hold situation. The <BREAK> key can be used to stop a program at any time but may result in loss of the program. It virtually resets the system and should be used with care.

INPUT

Previously there was a brief introduction to the keyword LET whose function was to assign values to variables at the stage of typing in a program before running it. However, it would be very useful if one could assign values to variables while a program is running.

The INPUT statement allows for such a facility and causes the computer to stop (during computation) and display "?". At this point the computer is asking for data to be typed in and any data entered at this stage is given to the named variable in the INPUT statement, for example:

```
 5 REM INPUT PROGRAM(1)
10 INPUT X
20 PRINT X
30 END
```

```
RUN

 ?47
           47
```

```
 5 REM INPUT PROGRAM(2)
10 INPUT"WHAT IS YOUR NAME ",NAME$
20 PRINT
30 PRINT"HELLO ",NAME$
40 PRINT
50 PRINT"NICE TO MAKE YOUR
   ACQUAINTANCE"
```

In Program (2) the computer asks for name of person. After it is entered in, the computer responds with:

HELLO [name of person] and
NICE TO MAKE YOUR ACQUAINTANCE

```
 5 REM INPUT PROGRAM (3)
10 INPUT"TYPE IN 3 No's ";N1,N2,N3
20 SUM=N1+N2+N3
30 PRINT"THE SUM IS = ";SUM
40 END
```

In Program (3) the computer asks for three numbers. On typing in the numbers of your choice, the computer replies with the answer.

It is important to match the data typed in to the variable to which it is to be assigned and it is recommended to include a written comment or some textual information associated with the input prompt for data, as in line 10 above.

DATA

A facility exists in BASIC which allows for large amounts of data to be held within a program. Numeric and string data may be held in a compact form usually at the end of a program. Items of data are held in the form of a list with each item separated from the next by a comma. It is a simple matter for information stored in this way to be altered, added to or deleted.

READ

DATA statements can therefore be thought of as blocks of data internal to the program. The assignment of these blocks of data to variables during program execution is achieved by READ statements which will name the variables to which an item of data is to be assigned. Thus, a numeric value is given to a numeric variable, and a string is given to a string variable.

```
  10 REM READ/DATA PROGRAM (1)
  20 LET A=3
  30 READ X,Y,Z
  40 PRINT
  50 LET B=A*X
  60 LET C=A*Y
  70 LET D=A*Z
  80 PRINT B,C,D
 200 DATA 4,8,1

RUN

 12          24           3
```

```
   5 REM READ/DATA PROGRAM (2)
  10 CLS
  20 PRINT" ** NAMES ** "
  30 PRINT:PRINT
  40 READ A$,B$,C$,D$
  50 PRINT A$,',B$,',C$,',D$
 100 DATA JOHN,GEORGE,SUE,DAVID
```

```
RUN

     ** NAMES **


    JOHN
    GEORGE
    SUE
    DAVID
```

Leave out DAVID in line 100 and the machine will respond with:

```
OUT OF DATA LINE 40
```

since the computer cannot find a data item for D$ in line 40.

Also note the inclusion of CLS in line 10. This clears the screen when the program is RUN and makes it easier to read.

```
10 REM DATA ASSIGNMENT PROG.(3)
20 READ A$,A
30 PRINT A$,A
40 DATA 29,JOHN
```

```
RUN
```

The computer will respond with:

```
NO SUCH VARIABLE AT LINE 20
```

Program (3) demonstrates an incorrect data assignment, i.e., mixing numeric and string variables.

When correct, output will be as below:

```
JOHN            29
```

NB: Data is read in strict order, one item after another.

RESTORE

A RESTORE statement is used to restore the data pointer to the beginning of the data block, thus enabling the next READ encountered to reassign data from the beginning of the sequence, for example:

```
  10 REM RESTORE PROG.(1)
  15 CLS
  20 READ A,B,C,D
  30 PRINT A,B,C,D
  40 RESTORE
  50 READ X,Y,Z
  60 PRINT X,Y,Z
 100 DATA 1,2,3,4,5,6,7,8,9
```

```
RUN

 1             2             3             4
 1             2             3
```

Restore Program (2) shows what happens when RESTORE is omitted, i.e. line 40:

```
  10 REM RESTORE PROG.(2)
  20 CLS
  30 READ A,B,C,D
  40 PRINT A,B,C,D
  50 READ X,Y,Z
  60 PRINT X,Y,Z
 100 DATA 1,2,3,4,5,6,7,8,9
```

```
RUN

 1             2             3             4
 5             6             7
```

GOTO

This statement causes the computer to jump to another program line, i.e. to another instruction. This then changes the program sequence and is called an Unconditional Statement or Unconditional Jump.

If too many GOTO statements are used in a program, it complicates the logic and makes it very difficult for the program sequence to be followed. It is recommended therefore, that a more structured method be adopted when writing programs and the number of GOTOs used be kept to a minimum, for example:

```
2Ø IF X=25 THEN GOTO 11Ø
```

ON ... GOTO

If you want to jump to one of a number of lines in accordance with certain conditions, the statement ON ... GOTO will achieve this and allow a jump to one of a number of lines depending on the value of the variable, for example:

```
1ØØ ON A GOTO 1Ø,2Ø,3Ø,4Ø,5Ø
```

This causes a jump to:

Line 10 if A = 1
Line 20 if A = 2
Line 30 if A = 3
Line 40 if A = 4
Line 50 if A = 5

and causes an error if A<1 or A>5.

IF ... THEN

IF ... THEN allows the computer to make a decision. If the condition given by IF is satisfied then the computer will carry out the instruction in accordance with the THEN message. If the condition is not satisfied the computer will move on to the next instruction, for example:

```
 5 REM IF....THEN PROG(1)
 6 CLS
10 INPUT"INPUT A NUMBER "X
20 PRINT
30 IF X=42 THEN 50←Conditional statement
40 GOTO 10←————Unconditional statement
50 PRINT"GOOD GUESS"
60 END
```

NB: If the number typed in is equal to 42 then the IF condition is satisfied and the computer will jump to line 50 in accordance with the THEN instruction, otherwise the computer asks for another number.

The IF ... THEN statement makes good use of Relational Operators and forms the Conditional Statement that allows for computer decisions to be made. Example program lines are shown below:

```
(a) 110 IF X<>Y THEN 240
(b) 20  IF PRICE<40 THEN 100
(c) 10 IF MARKS<75 AND>60 THEN 200
(d) 75 IF ANSWER=YES THEN PRINT"GOOD"
```

An extension to the IF ... THEN statement is provided for by the addition of ELSE which allows an alternative course of action to be taken. This is best explained with the aid of the following – change line 30 in Program (1) on page 15 to:

```
30 IF X=42 THEN 50 ELSE 10
```

NB: Delete line 40.

Another example:

```
 1 REM IF....THEN PROG.(2)
 5 CLS
10 INPUT"INPUT A NUMBER "X
20 PRINT'''''''''''''''''''''''''
30 IF X<30 THEN PRINT"TOO SMALL"
40 IF X=42 THEN FORA=1 TO 100:
   PRINT"CORRECT....GOOD GUESS":
   NEXT:END
50 IF X>50 THEN PRINT"TOO LARGE"
60 GOTO 10
```

Program (2) contains Relational Operators and printed messages within the IF ... THEN statements. Line 20 uses the apostrophe to skip lines, thus printing messages and prompts at the top and bottom of the VDU/TV screen. Line 40 rewards a correct guess with the printing of the message:

```
CORRECT....GOOD GUESS
```

100 times in list format. This is achieved using a Count Controlled Loop (FOR ... NEXT), which determines the number

of times the message appears. Line 40 is known as a Multi-statement line, having four statements separated by colons.

The Flowchart

At this stage in introducing BASIC programming techniques it may be helpful as an aid to understanding program development to introduce flowcharts. Flowcharts provide a pictorial method of showing the step-by-step sequence to a computer program and is useful as an aid to program development. Basically, four different shaped boxes are used:

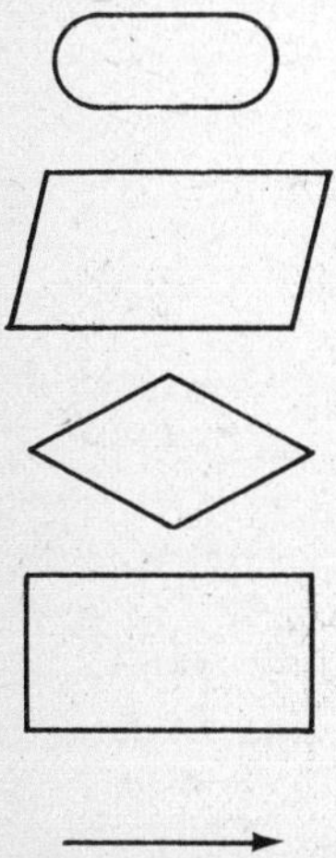

Start/stop

Input/Output

Decisions

Activity

Direction of flow

A flowchart should be used when developing a computer program to record in block structure the step-by-step process used to solve a problem. One procedure for computer program development is as follows:

(i) Thoroughly understand the problem;
(ii) Decide on Input and Output data required;
(iii) Draw flowchart showing logic used to solve problem;
(iv) Translate flowchart into coded instructions, i.e. program.

Example Flowchart for Program (2), page 16

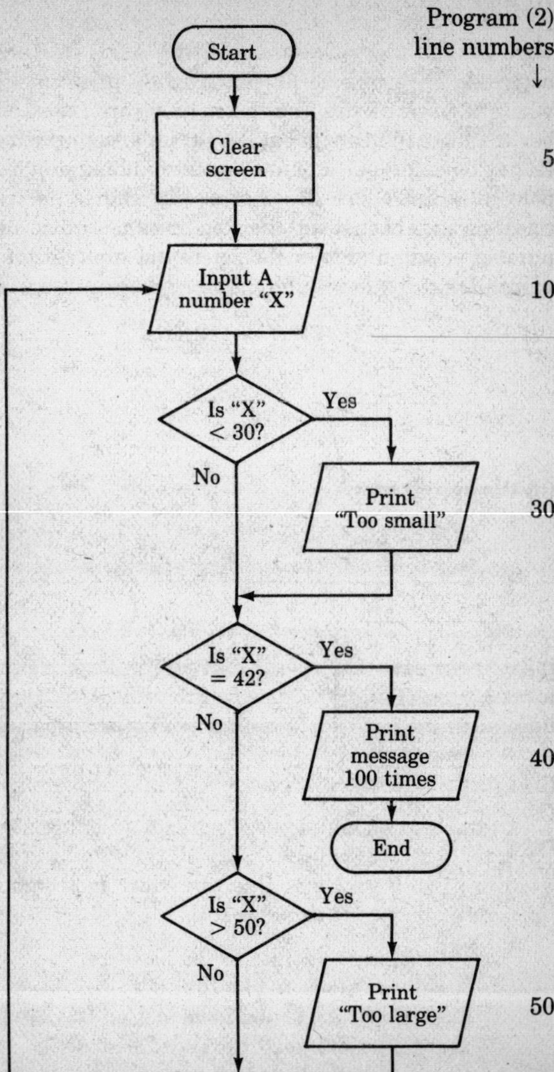

Loops

At the beginning of the book it was stated that computers were good at carrying out repetitive tasks. In BASIC these activities are achieved by constructing program loops, i.e., where a group of program instructions are repeated a number of times. Whilst it is easy to set up a loop which is never-ending or perpetual, it is more important and provides a very powerful BASIC technique, to control these activities by counting the repetitions or by leaving the loop at a specified number or when certain conditions are met. Techniques involved are:

(i) Perpetual loops;
(ii) Count controlled loops;
(iii) Condition controlled loops;
(iv) Nested loops.

(i) Perpetual loops

```
 5 REM GOTO LOOP(1)
10 PRINT"THIS IS A LOOP";
20 GOTO 10
```

Line 20 causes the program to loop back to line 10, creating a never-ending screen-full of scrolling text. Exit from the loop may be obtained by pressing the <ESCAPE> key. GOTO unconditionally transfers control to another program line.

(ii) Count controlled loops

Count controlled loops are such that the computer counts the repetitions of a given activity. Starting with the first, it adds one for each subsequent activity until a set value is reached. A flowchart can best depict this process. (*See* next page.)

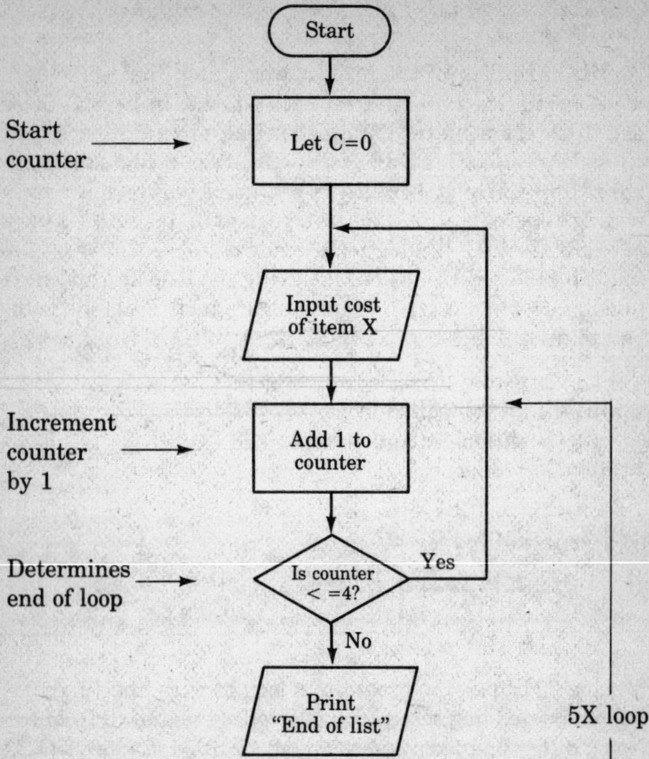


```
 5 REM COUNT CONTROLLED LOOP
 6 REM PROGRAM (1)
10 CLS
20 C=0
30 INPUT"COST OF ITEM ="X
40 PRINT
50 C=C+1
60 IF C <= 4 THEN 30
70 PRINT "END OF LIST"
80 END
```

NB: Line 60 reads IFC <= 4 THEN 30 because computer counts from 0 not 1, i.e., 0 to 4 = 5.

```
RUN

    COST OF ITEM =56.00

    COST OF ITEM =42.98

    COST OF ITEM =23.00

    COST OF ITEM =98.34

    COST OF ITEM =47.50

    END OF LIST
```

Program (2) provides another example of a count controlled loop. It prints out the powers of "X" controlled by loop variable "J":

```
  1 REM COUNT CONTROLLED LOOP
  2 REM PROGRAM (2)
  5 CLS
 10 INPUT"TYPE IN A No. ",X
 20 PRINT:PRINT:PRINT:PRINT
 30 PRINT"          POWERS OF ";X
 35 PRINT:PRINT
 40 J=0
 50 T=1
 60 PRINT X;" TO THE POWER ";
    J;" IS ";T
 70 T=T*X
 80 J=J+1
 90 IF J <= 10 THEN 60
100 END
```

Result of RUNning Program (2):

```
TYPE IN A No.?2



          POWERS OF 2

             2 TO THE POWER 0 IS 1
             2 TO THE POWER 1 IS 2
             2 TO THE POWER 2 IS 4
             2 TO THE POWER 3 IS 8
             2 TO THE POWER 4 IS 16
             2 TO THE POWER 5 IS 32
             2 TO THE POWER 6 IS 64
             2 TO THE POWER 7 IS 128
             2 TO THE POWER 8 IS 256
             2 TO THE POWER 9 IS 512
             2 TO THE POWER 10 IS 1024
```

FOR ... NEXT loop

The FOR ... NEXT loop is another technique used by BASIC to obtain repetition of a block of lines within a program. The FOR ... NEXT method of loop control is similar to the previous Count Controlled loop, however, the number of repetitions is controlled by the values given to the loop variable along with defined incremental steps. These instructions make up one line and the NEXT statement returns control to the FOR statement enclosing the program lines to be repeated, for example:

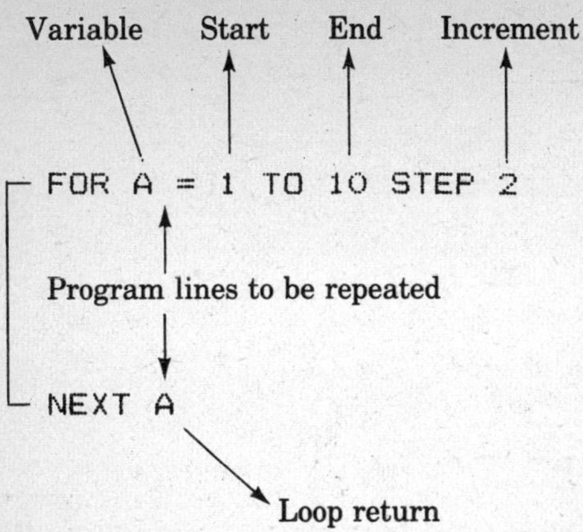

Example program:

```
  5 REM FOR....NEXT PROG(1)
 10 CLS
 20 FOR A=1 TO 10 STEP 1
 30 PRINT A
 40 NEXT A
 50 END

RUN

  1
  2
  3
  4
  5
  6
  7
  8
  9
 10
```

NB: If the STEP function is not defined the computer assumes it to be 1. Incremental steps may be negative, positive or fractional, e.g., replace line 20 above with:

```
20 FOR A=1 TO 10 STEP 2
```

```
RUN

  1
  3
  5
  7
  9
```

or with:

```
20 FOR A=10 TO 1 STEP -1
```

```
RUN

 10
  9
  8
  7
  6
  5
  4
  3
  2
  1
```

Finally, replace line 20 with:

```
20 FOR A=1 TO 10 STEP 0.5
```

```
RUN

    1
  1.5
    2
  2.5
    3
  3.5
```

etc.

The following program illustrates one practical use for the FOR ... NEXT loop where it provides a very useful and neat way of achieving a running total for costing items or for any application where a cumulative result is required:

```
  5 REM FOR....NEXT LOOP PROG(2)
 10 REM RUNNING TOTAL PROG.
 20 CLS
 30 PRINT"ENTER No.    NUMBER","TOTAL"
 40 T=0
 50 FOR A=1 TO 10
 60 INPUT N
 70 T=T+N
 80 PRINT"  ",N,T
 90 NEXT A
100 PRINT:PRINT
110 PRINT"TOTAL=";T
120 END
```

(iii) Condition controlled loops

The REPEAT ... UNTIL loop creates a situation in a BASIC program where a specified group of program lines are repeated until a set condition is satisfied, for example:

```
 1 REM REPEAT....UNTIL LOOP PROG(1)
 5 CLS
10 REPEAT
20 INPUT"TYPE IN NAME ",NAME$
30 PRINT:PRINT:PRINT
40 PRINT"THAT'S A NICE NAME"
50 PRINT'''''''''''''''''
60 UNTIL NAME$="JOE BLOGGS":
   PRINT"THAT NAME IS FAMILIAR"
   :END
```

Program (1) above, allows any name to be entered in and will continue to ask for names until "JOE BLOGGS" is typed in, thereby satisfying the UNTIL statement in line 60 and terminating the program.

Program (2) below, invites one to type in a number between 1 and 10. The computer responds by displaying the number chosen (X), X plus 2, X minus 2, X divided by 2, and X multiplied by 2. The program ceases to run when 7 is typed in:

```
5 REM REPEAT....UNTIL LOOP PROG(2)
10 CLS
20 REPEAT
30 INPUT"INSERT A NUMBER BETWEEN
   1 AND 10 ",X
40 PRINT''''''''''
50 PRINTX,',X+2,',X-2,',X/2,',X*2
60 PRINT''''
70 UNTIL X=7:PRINT"THIS IS THE
   END OF THE PROGRAM"
```

(iv) Nested loops

The REPEAT ... UNTIL loop together with the FOR ... NEXT loop provides BBC BASIC with powerful and well-structured programming techniques. The use of these techniques is further enhanced by another useful technique in which loops are "nested", i.e., a loop or loops within a loop, for example:

```
5 REM NESTED LOOPS PROG(1)
10 FOR A = 1 TO 10
20 FOR B = 1 TO A
30 PRINT"TOM ";
40 NEXT B
50 PRINT
60 NEXT A
70 END
```

Program (1) consists of two loops, an outer loop (A) and an inner loop denoted by the variable (B). The value of the outer loop governs the range of values of the inner loop. All types of loops may be nested if required, however, it is important to take great care when nesting loops in a complex program in order to prevent overlapping. A nested loop must be completely within another loop or completely outside it. For example, the loops shown below are illegal and the computer will indicate so:

```
┌─ 10 FOR A = 1 TO 10
┼─ 20 FOR B = 1 TO A
│    - - - - - - -
│    - - - - - - -
│    - - - -   -        ←——Loops overlapping
│    -   - - -   -
│
└─ 80 NEXT A
└─ 90 NEXT B
```

The program should be as follows:

```
┌── 10 FOR A = 1 TO 10
│┌─ 20 FOR B = 1 TO A
││     - - - - - - -
││     - - - - -  - -
││     - - - - - -
││      - -  - -  - -
││
│└─ 80 NEXT B
└── 90 NEXT A
```

Program (2) on the next page uses several loops and some are nested. The program listing is designed to print the morse code symbol for S O S, three times above the corresponding letters:

```
  1 REM NESTED LOOPS PROG(2)
  5 CLS
 10 FOR M = 1 TO 3
 11 PRINT
 20 FOR A =1 TO 3
 30 PRINT" .";
 40 NEXT A
 50 FOR B = 1 TO 3
 60 PRINT" -";
 70 NEXT B
 80 FOR C = 1 TO 3
 90 PRINT" .";
100 NEXT C
110 NEXT M
111 PRINT:PRINT
120 FOR D = 1 TO 3
130 PRINT"  S      O      S"
140 NEXT D
150 END

RUN
```

Loop A prints 3 dots

Loop B prints 3 dashes

Loop C prints 3 dots

```
 . . . - - - . . .
 . . . - - - . . .
 . . . - - - . . .
```

Loop M prints loops A, B & C 3 times, i.e. · · ·——— · ·

```
  S      O      S
  S      O      S
  S      O      S
```

Loop D prints S O S 3 times

Subroutines and Procedures

(i) Subroutines

A subroutine is a group of lines which are separated or outside the main program and may be called upon from time to time during execution of the main program by means of the statement GOSUB. This subsection or subroutine can then be called at a number of different places in the main program, eliminating the need for repetition of the same group of lines within the main program.

The end of a subroutine is indicated by the keyword RETURN which returns control to the main program at the next statement following the GOSUB, for example:

```
  5 REM SUBROUTINE PROG.
 10 CLS
 20 GOSUB 150
 30 PRINT:PRINT
 40 INPUT"TYPE IN ONE OF
    THESE EVEN NUMBERS
    AND PRESS RETURN ",A
 50 PRINT:PRINT:PRINT
 60 CLS
 70 GOSUB 150
 80 PRINT:PRINT
 90 INPUT"TYPE IN ANOTHER
    EVEN NUMBER ",B:CLS
100 PRINT;;;;;;;;;;;
110 LET C=A+B
120 PRINT"SUM OF 1st AND
    2nd EVEN NUMBERS = ";C
130 END
140 REM GOSUB"5 EVEN No's"
150 PRINT" 5 EVEN NUMBERS"
160 PRINT
170 FOR N=2 TO 10 STEP 2
180 PRINT N
190 NEXT N
200 RETURN
```

(ii) Procedures

Procedures are basically the same as Subroutines except for a few differences which are listed below:

(a) Procedures are *named* as opposed to Subroutines which are referred to by line numbers;
(b) Procedures are called by PROCname instead of by a GOSUB line number;
(c) Procedures have to be defined and start with a DEFPROC name and the procedure is terminated with the keyword ENDPROC.

Procedures, like subroutines, must not be defined within the body of a program and should be placed in a section, usually at the end of a program, which is not executed.

The use of procedures enables the programmer to structure BASIC programs in blocks or modules which are easier to handle and understand. Programming is thus made more straightforward; problems can be broken down into smaller sections or modules, perhaps with the aid of a flowchart, and handled individually until the entire program is written.

NB: All variables used in procedures should be declared as "LOCAL" (keyword) variables in order to protect the value given to a similarly named variable if used in the main program.

The program on the next page illustrates the use of procedures and compares their use with the subroutines used in a similar program on page 29:

```
  5 REM PROCEDURE PROG.
 10 CLS
 20 PROCnumbers
 30 PRINT:PRINT
 40 INPUT"TYPE IN ONE
    OF THESE EVEN NUMBERS
    AND PRESS RETURN ",A
 50 PRINT:PRINT:PRINT
 60 CLS
 70 PROCnumbers
 80 PRINT:PRINT
 90 INPUT"TYPE IN ANOTHER
    EVEN NUMBER ",B:CLS
100 PRINT'''''''''''
110 LET C=A+B
120 PRINT"SUM OF 1st AND
    2nd EVEN NUMBERS = ";C
130 END
140 REM PROCEDURE DEFINED
150 DEF PROCnumbers
160 PRINT "5 EVEN NUMBERS"
170 PRINT
180 FOR N=2 TO 10 STEP 2
190 PRINT N
200 NEXT N
210 ENDPROC
```

NB: The program line 130 preceding the subroutine/procedure should be an END statement in order to prevent the main program section from going into the sub/procedure section.

The advantage gained in using procedures, as opposed to subroutines, is to obtain an overall more structured program. Lines 20 and 70 immediately refer to a named procedure instead of just a line number and reference to lines 150 to 210 show the actual defined procedure; the procedure module commencing with the identifying name, DEF PROCnumbers (define procedure called numbers), and terminates with the keyword ENDPROC (end of procedure).

Procedures also enhance program simplicity and make them more readable and easy to follow.

The size of the above program does not warrant the use of either procedures or subroutines and is only included to illustrate their use.

Arrays

Various methods of placing information into a computer have been discussed when introducing the keywords, LET, INPUT and READ/DATA. These methods provide a facility for assigning single variables with either numerical or textual data or in the case of READ/DATA statements they assign a number of different variables with data that is usually related, i.e., a list of names, examination results, list of stock items, etc.

However, it is more often than not that a large amount of data is required to be stored or processed by a microcomputer and this data is usually in list format, as indeed is a large amount of the data handled by a computer, e.g., bank account information, names, addresses and telephone numbers, lists of stock items, etc.

Computer data in the form of groups or lists are called Arrays and BASIC provides a convenient way of handling such arrays. The variable letter or name is common throughout the array whilst each element of the array is identified by a unique number enclosed in the parentheses or brackets immediately following the variable name. These are called Subscripted Variables, for example:

```
String variable                    Numeric variable
         ↓                            ↙
         A$(1)                A(1)
             ↖                ↗
               Subscript
```

The list of children's names on the next page illustrates the use of subscripted variables in a one-dimensional array:

```
A$(1)"PAUL"
A$(2)"SARA"
A$(3)"ANDREW"
A$(4)"JANE"
A$(5)"THOMAS"
A$(6)"SUSAN"
```

A six-element string array

Before using arrays the computer must be told the size of the list or array so that it can allocate sufficient memory space to accommodate the array of data. This is achieved by using the keyword DIM, short for dimension, it states the size and name of the array and in BBC BASIC should be used to declare all arrays irrespective of size. A suitable DIM statement for the above list of names would be as follows:

```
DIM NAME$(6)
```

NB: In the program to follow there are six children's names, denoted by NAME$(0) to NAME$(5), i.e., DIM NAME$(6) reserves 6 elements starting with NAME$(0).

Program (1) prints out the list of children's names as read from the data statements and also prints the list in reverse order:

```
  1 REM ARRAY PROG(1)
  5 CLS
 10 DIM NAME$(6)
 20 FOR A = 0 TO 5
 30 READ NAME$
 40 NAME$(A)=NAME$
 50 PRINTTAB(12);A,NAME$(A)
 60 NEXT A
 70 PRINT
 80 FOR A = 5 TO 0 STEP -1
 90 PRINTTAB(12);A,NAME$(A)
100 NEXT A
110 DATA PAUL,SARA,ANDREW
120 DATA JANE,THOMAS,SUSAN
```

```
RUN

  0        PAUL
  1        SARA
  2        ANDREW
  3        JANE
  4        THOMAS
  5        SUSAN

  5        SUSAN
  4        THOMAS
  3        JANE
  2        ANDREW
  1        SARA
  0        PAUL
```

The previous example demonstrates a typical one-dimensional array whilst the second program prints out three sets of data. The DIM statement has two numbers, the first indicating the number of rows and the second the number of columns, i.e., DIM SALARY (11,2). Remember BBC BASIC starts counting at zero, therefore 11 will refer to twelve rows, and 2 to three columns. Since DIM has two subscripts, then it is called a Two-dimensional Array:

```
   1 REM ARRAY PROG (2)
   5 CLS
  10 DIM SALARY(11,2)
  20 RESTORE 1000
  30 FOR M=0 TO 11
  40 FOR J=0 TO 2
  50 READ SALARY(M,J)
  60 NEXT J
  70 NEXT M
  80 PRINT"         MONTH    EARNINGS
       NET"
  90 FOR J=0 TO 11
 100 FOR C=0 TO 2
 110 PRINT SALARY(J,C);
```

```
120 NEXT C
130 PRINT
140 NEXT J
150 END
1000 DATA 1,510,340,2,508,337,3
     ,486,303,4,492,328
1010 DATA 5,491,326,6,511,341,7
     ,507,339,8,494,327
1020 DATA 9,502,334,10,481,300,11
     ,501,333,12,479,329
```

Result of RUNning Program (2):

```
MONTH    EARNINGS     NET
  1        510        340
  2        508        337
  3        486        303
  4        492        328
  5        491        326
  6        511        341
  7        507        339
  8        494        327
  9        502        334
 10        481        300
 11        501        333
 12        479        329
```

Simple Sort Procedures

Lists of numerical and alphabetical information are usually best tabulated in ascending/descending or alphabetical order so as to simplify the searching, handling and filing of such data.

The use of arrays simplifies the manipulation of data in a list, for example, it was a simple matter to print out the children's names in reverse order in the Array Program (1), page 33.

To sort data into alphabetical or numerical order is a simple matter for the computer since all keyboard characters are allocated a number code (refer to the section on String Variables) which puts numbers into ascending order and letters into alphabetical order, i.e.,

Keyboard characters

```
1,2,3 ...      A,B,C ...      a,b,c ...
```

ASCII code numbers

```
49,50,51 ...   65,66,67 ...   97,98,99 ...
```

One simple method used to sort data in an array is to compare two items using the IF ... THEN statement. If, for example, line 90 compares two strings, i.e.,

```
90 IF A$(1)< A$(3) THEN ...
```

and A$(1) is less than A$(3) then the comparison is true and the program continues to compare the first item with the third, fourth and so on, until a false condition exists, in which case, the two items are swopped over, thus satisfying the order format.

This compare-and-swop procedure continues until the entire list of data has been sorted into alphabetical or numerical order.

The simple step-by-step procedure of a numeric "sort" routine is given below. (A similar procedure may be used for literal data.) Example:

Sort four numbers, 2, 3, 9 and 7 into ascending order.

If 1st number < 2nd number then true, else swop.

	1st	*2nd*	*3rd*	*4th*	*Array Positions*
1st run	2	3	9	7	1st No. compared with all others. 2 is smallest No. and therefore remains in 1st position.

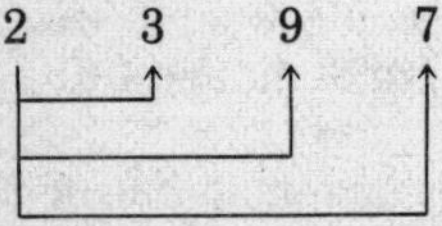

2nd run	2	3	9	7	2nd No. compared with remaining Nos. Since it is less than these it remains in position 2.

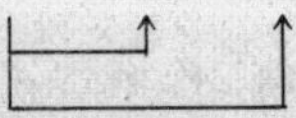

3rd run	2	3	9	7	3rd comparison. Here 9 is > 7, therefore a swop must take place. (*See below*)
	2	3	7	9 ←	Situation after interchange.

The process of interchange is shown below with the aid of the following diagram:

X = temporary memory locations

	Memory locations A	B	X
Swop over the data in memory locations A and B →	9	7	
1st step: Let X=A →	9	7	9
2nd step: Let A=B →	7	7	9
3rd step: Let B=X →	7	9	9

Here the contents of memory locations A and B have been swopped around.

Sample Program – the program below sorts ten numbers into numerical order:

```
  5 REM NUMERICAL SORT PROG(1)
 10 CLS
 20 DIM NUM(9)
 30 FOR J=0 TO 9
 40 INPUT"INSERT YOUR NUMBER "NUM(J)
 50 PRINT
 60 NEXT J
 70 FOR J=0 TO 8
 80 FOR K=J+1 TO 9                        ← Compare
 90 IF NUM(J)<NUM(K) THEN 110
100 R=NUM(J):NUM(J)=NUM(K):NUM(K)=R
110 NEXT K:NEXT J                         ← Interchange
```

```
120 CLS
130 FOR J=0 TO 9
140 PRINT J,NUM(J)
150 NEXT J
```

Numerical Sort Program RUNning:

```
INSERT YOUR NUMBER 45

INSERT YOUR NUMBER 677

INSERT YOUR NUMBER 23

INSERT YOUR NUMBER 450

INSERT YOUR NUMBER 231

INSERT YOUR NUMBER 983

INSERT YOUR NUMBER 36

INSERT YOUR NUMBER 30

INSERT YOUR NUMBER 2

INSERT YOUR NUMBER 78
```

Result of Numerical Sort Program:

```
0              2
1             23
2             30
3             36
4             45
5             78
6            231
7            450
8            677
9            983
```

String Manipulation

Throughout the book we have used strings made up of letters, numbers and punctuation which can be up to 255 characters long. The dollar sign ($) at the end of the group of characters indicates a string and BBC BASIC provides a selection of string functions which allow the programmer to manipulate and rearrange strings. One typical application where string manipulation is employed is Word Processing.

The following is a selection of string functions as used in BBC BASIC, with examples to illustrate their function.

LEN

(Abbreviation of length) indicates the number of characters in a string, i.e., a string function that produces a numeric result, for example:

```
   5 REM LEN PROG
  10 LET X = LEN("MONDAY")
  20 PRINT X

RUN

  6
```

RIGHT$

Copies a specified number of characters at the right-hand portion of a string, for example:

```
10 REM RIGHT$ PROG
20 CLS
30 LET X$=RIGHT$("21st APRIL,1947",4)
40 PRINTTAB(16,10);X$

RUN

  1947
```

LEFT$

Reproduces a specified number of characters at the left-hand portion of a string, for example:

```
 5 REM LEFT$ PROG
10 LET A$="PROGRAMMING"
20 PRINT LEFT$(A$,7)

RUN

PROGRAM
```

MID$

This is rather more sophisticated than the previous string functions and extracts and copies portions of strings from a specified starting point, for example:

```
10 PRINT MID$("MANAGEMENT",4,3)

RUN

AGE

10 PRINT MID$("MANAGEMENT",5,3)

RUN

GEM

10 N$ = "NTJEM"
20 FOR NAME = 1 TO 4
30 PRINT MID$(N$,2,NAME)
40 NEXT NAME

RUN

T
TJ
TJE
TJEM
```

The following program illustrates the use of LEN and MID$ functions in order to code simple messages. The coded sentence is produced by replacing every fifth letter in the alphabet with an asterisk and then printing it out in reverse order:

```
 10 REM STRING MANIPULATION PROG.
 20 CLS
 30 DIM A$(30),L$(6)
 40 L$(1)="A"
 50 L$(2)="E"
 60 L$(3)="J"
 70 L$(4)="O"
 80 L$(5)="T"
 81 L$(6)="Y"
 85 PRINTTAB(12,6);"* CIPHER *"
 90 REM NOT MORE THAN 30 CHARACTERS
100 INPUT'''"SENTENCE ", S$
110 FOR A=1 TO LEN(S$)
120 A$(A)=MID$(S$,A,1)
130 FOR B=1 TO 6
140 IF A$(A)=L$(B) THEN A$(A)="*"
150 NEXT B
160 C$=C$+A$(A)+"  "
170 NEXT A
180 C$=C$+"!!!!"
190 PRINT''C$
200 FOR A=LEN(S$) TO 1 STEP -1
210 D$=D$+A$(A)
220 NEXT A
230 PRINT''D$
240 END
```

RUN

Example:
Type in "JACK AND JILL WENT UP THE HILL"

NB: A space is considered a character.

Result of String Manipulation Program

```
* CIPHER *


SENTENCE ?JACK AND JILL WENT UP THE HILL


* * C K  * N D  * I L L  W * N *  U P  * H *  H I L L !!!!


LLIH *H* PU *N*W LLI* DN* KC**
```

VAL

This turns a string into a number (provided the string contents are numeric), for example:

```
VAL("1952") = 1952

VAL("NUMBER") = 0
```

The main use is to validate input data, for example:

```
 5 REM VAL PROG
10 CLS
20 INPUT"TYPE IN YOUR NAME "NAME$
30 IF VAL(NAME$)<>0 THEN 10
40 PRINT:PRINT
50 PRINTNAME$
```

Line 20 expects the input to be a string, e.g., JOHN, however, if a number key is pressed in error then line 30 cancels the input and returns the program to line 20 prompting the input of your name again.

STR$

The STR$ function is opposite to that of VAL, i.e., it turns the number that follows it into a string, so that it can be used as a string instead of a number, for example:

```
STR$(12345) = "12345"
```

The use can best be demonstrated with the aid of the following program which prints a long variable number in the centre of the screen:

```
10 LET A$=STR$(113233471)
20 PRINTTAB(16,10);A$
```

INSTR

This allows one to search for a string contained within another string, for example, we can use it to test whether or not the string "TRON" is contained in the string "ELECTRONICS", for example:

```
PRINT INSTR("ELECTRONICS","TRON")
```

The result printed out will be "5", which indicates that the second string "TRON" is indeed held within (substring) the first string "ELECTRONICS".

Note that the response would be "0", meaning "no" if the second string was not found to be held within the first string, for example:

```
PRINT INSTR("ELECTRONICS","UTRON")
```

NB: The first string must always be longer than the second and a space is not allowed after INSTR.

STRING$

This provides for the duplication of strings or for producing one long string by joining together duplicate short strings, for example:

```
10 LET A$=STRING$(3,"HELLO ")
20 PRINT A$

RUN

HELLO HELLO HELLO
```

or:

```
10 LET SPACE$=STRING$(20," ")
20 PRINT SPACE$;"END OF LINE"

RUN

                    END OF LINE
<------------------>
    (20 spaces)
```

The BBC Micro holds all data, i.e. letters, numbers, punctuation and symbols in the form of a number code. This code is called the American Standard Code for Information Interchange (ASCII), and is an attempt by computer manufacturers to standardise on an alphanumerical and symbolic number code which should give some compatibility between computers and their documentation, etc.

A list of ASCII codes is given on page 46.

There are two string functions which allow conversion between a character and its ASCII code:

(i) ASC(A$)
which gives the ASCII code of the first character in the string held in parentheses, i.e., A$, for example:

```
PRINT ASC("ALPHA")
65                    (65 is the ASCII code for "A")

PRINT ASC("ZULU")
90                    (90 is the ASCII code for "Z")
```

(ii) CHR$
This is the opposite of ASC(A$) and converts an ASCII code number into its equivalent character or symbol, for example:

```
PRINT CHR$(65)
```

Print out = A

The program below prints out the characters converted from the ASCII codes 32 to 127. (*See* page 46 for a list of these codes and related characters.):

```
10 FOR C=32 TO 127
20 PRINT C;" ";CHR$(C)
25 X=GET
30 NEXT C
```

The previous program contains a new word, GET, at program line 25. Its function is to stop and hold the program, allowing the user to read the ASCII code and related character. To proceed with the program any key may be pressed and the next ASCII code and character will be displayed.

NB: When a key is pressed after a certain waiting period the ASCII code of that key will be assigned to the variable associated with GET.

The following program combines the ASC, CHR$, LEN and MID$ functions to provide a useful utility program for changing a short sentence in Upper Case letters to Lower Case:

```
 5 REM UPPER TO LOWER CASE PROG
10 CLS
20 INPUT"TYPE IN SHORT SENTENCE ",S$
30 FOR A = 1 TO LEN(S$)
40 L=ASC(MID$(S$,A,1))
50 IF L>64 AND L<91 THEN L=L+32
60 LAST$=LAST$+CHR$(L)
70 NEXT A
80 PRINT LAST$
```

If L = Capital Letters A–Z then L = Lower Case letters

Result of Upper to Lower Case Program:

```
TYPE IN SHORT SENTENCE ?
                  MARY HAD A LITTLE LAMB
mary had a little lamb
```

NB: To change from Upper Case to Lower Case requires that 32 be added to the ASCII code for each letter.

ASCII Codes (Mode 7)

(American Standard Code for Information Interchange)

32	SPACE	64	@	96	£
33	!	65	A	97	a
34	"	66	B	98	b
35	#	67	C	99	c
36	$	68	D	100	d
37	%	69	E	101	e
38	&	70	F	102	f
39	'	71	G	103	g
40	(	72	H	104	h
41	)	73	I	105	i
42	*	74	J	106	j
43	+	75	K	107	k
44	,	76	L	108	l
45	-	77	M	109	m
46	.	78	N	110	n
47	/	79	O	111	o
48	0	80	P	112	p
49	1	81	Q	113	q
50	2	82	R	114	r
51	3	83	S	115	s
52	4	84	T	116	t
53	5	85	U	117	u
54	6	86	V	118	v
55	7	87	W	119	w
56	8	88	X	120	x
57	9	89	Y	121	y
58	:	90	Z	122	z
59	;	91	←	123	¼
60	<	92	½	124	‖
61	=	93	→	125	¾
62	>	94	↑	126	÷
63	?	95	_	127	DELETE

Program Planning Techniques

Beginners to computer programming usually have a tendency to begin writing the program instructions when invited to find a computer solution to a suggested problem without first analysing the problem and planning solutions initially on paper.

Of course, for short programs this may not be necessary but for long and complex programs where certain activities are repeated a great number of times and different activities and techniques are involved then some kind of organised, controlled planning must be used to develop and create an efficient and bug-free program.

A brief outline to a suggested program planning procedure was given previously and below a more detailed description of the steps involved is given. This is not meant to be a rigid structure but just a guide to be used when handling more involved computer programs as and when you become more competent at using BBC BASIC:

(i)

Thoroughly understand problem:
Define aims;
Understand concepts.

(ii)

(a) Output:
Information/results to be displayed on screen;
Format of output;
Text/graphics or both;
Any hard copies to be produced or data to be saved.

(b) Input:
Compile list of data to be used;
Methods of capturing data.

(iii)

Draw flowchart or list logical program steps in sequence:
Break down into manageable portions (modules), activities or jobs that the computer will have to

perform to process all data and produce the output required;

The order in which these activities are to be handled by the computer along with their frequency;

Complete the flowchart or list and include all modules of operations or activites that make up the step-by-step sequence of events to be carried out by the computer from start to finish.

(iv)

Translate flowchart into coded instructions:

BBC BASIC provides Procedures as an aid to modularising programs;

Use REM statements to name and explain various parts of the program, etc.;

Divide and clearly show location of Subroutines or Procedures;

Validate all data to be processed by the computer;

Reject all incorrect or unwanted data;

Program should be User-friendly, i.e., with plenty of screen messages to keep the User informed and provide information concerning operation of the program.

In conclusion to this brief introduction to BBC BASIC an example of a Stock Control Program is included. It has been developed using the above program planning techniques and employs procedures to obtain a very structured and simple modular design. It is intended as a demonstration program only and would therefore require many more procedures to be included in order to provide for a practical Stock Control application.

NB: In an attempt to validate input data program lines 205, 225 aand 335 have been included.

The procedure PROCwait is called from within two other procedures, namely PROCquantity and PROClist.

Sample Stock Control Program

```
 10 REM *** SAMPLE PROGRAM FOR A
    STOCK CONTROL APPLICATION ***
 40 DIM item$(20),quantity(20)
 50 PROCtitle
 60 PROClist
 70 PROCquantity
 80 PRINT''''''
 90 CLS
100 PROCoutputlist
110 END
120 REM**************************
130 DEF PROCtitle
140 PRINTTAB(12,1);"***************"
150 PRINTTAB(12,2);"* STOCK LIST *"
151 PRINTTAB(12,3);"***************"
160 PRINT''
170 ENDPROC
180 REM**************************
190 DEF PROClist
200 INPUT"please enter TOTAL number
    of items to be listed - maximum
    number 20",list
205 IF list<1 OR list>20 THEN 200
210 FOR A= 1 TO list
220 INPUT'"type in name of item "
    item$(A)
225 IF VAL(item$(A))<>0 THEN 220
230 NEXT A
240 PRINT''"   -THE LIST IS NOW
     COMPLETE-"
250 PROCwait
260 CLS
270 ENDPROC
280 REM***************************
290 DEF PROCquantity
```

```
291 PRINT"now type in QUANTITY
    against name of item"
292 PROCwait
293 CLS
300 FOR A=1 TO list
310 PRINT" the item is ";item$(A)
320 PRINT''''
330 INPUT"now type in quantity
    ",quantity(A)
335 IF quantity(A)<1 OR quantity(A)
    > 20 THEN 330
340 CLS
350 NEXT A
360 PRINT''"  -THAT COMPLETES LIST-"
370 PROCwait
380 CLS
390 ENDPROC
400 REM*****************************
410 DEF PROCoutputlist
420 PRINT'''
430 PRINT"No.","ITEMS","   QUANTITY"
440 PRINT"===","=====","   ========"
450 PRINT
460 FOR A=1 TO list
470 PRINT;A,item$(A),quantity(A)
480 NEXT A
490 ENDPROC
500 REM****************************
510 DEF PROCwait
520 PRINT''"++ PRESS THE SPACE
    BAR NOW ++"
530 Z=GET
540 ENDPROC
```

Program lines 40 to 110 form the main body of the program. Line 40 dimensions or determines the length or size of the list. Lines 50, 60, 70 and 100 call the various Procedures in turn from printing the title of the program first

(PROCtitle), to printing the completed list on the screen (PROCoutputlist).

The END statement at line 110 serves to terminate the main body of the program and to prevent the main program instructions from running into the list of Procedures.

REM statements are used to separate and identify Procedures. All three main Procedures, namely PROClist, PROCquantity and PROCoutputlist employ the FOR ... NEXT loop in the first two instances to prompt the user for information concerning the stocklist, i.e., names and quantities if the items (using the INPUT statement), and finally to print the list on the screen in the procedure, PROCoutputlist.

The number of times the FOR ... NEXT loop is to be repeated is determined by the number assigned to the variable "list", the value of which is selected by the user at the beginning of the program and should not exceed 20 as set by the DIM statement, line 40.

Please note following is a list of other titles that are available in our range of Radio, Electronics and Computer Books.

These should be available from all good Booksellers, Radio Component Dealers and Mail Order Companies.

However, should you experience difficulty in obtaining any title in your area, then please write directly to the publisher enclosing payment to cover the cost of the book plus adequate postage.

If you would like a complete catalogue of our entire range of Radio, Electronics and Computer Books then please send a Stamped Addressed Envelope to:

BERNARD BABANI (publishing) LTD
THE GRAMPIANS
SHEPHERDS BUSH ROAD
LONDON W6 7NF
ENGLAND

160	Coil Design and Construction Manual	£1.95
202	Handbook of Integrated Circuits (IC's) Equivalents & Substitutes	£1.95
205	First Book of Hi-Fi Loudspeaker Enclosures	£0.95
208	Practical Stereo and Quadrophony Handbook	£0.75
214	Audio Enthusiasts Handbook	£0.85
219	Solid State Novelty Projects	£0.85
220	Build Your Own Solid State Hi-Fi and Audio Accessories	£0.85
221	28 Tested Transistor Projects	£1.25
222	Solid State Short Wave Receivers for Beginners	£1.95
223	50 Projects Using IC CA3130	£1.25
224	50 CMOS IC Projects	£1.35
225	A Practical Introduction to Digital IC's	£1.75
226	How to Build Advanced Short Wave Receivers	£1.95
227	Beginners Guide to Building Electronic Projects	£1.95
228	Essential Theory for the Electronics Hobbyist	£1.95
RCC	Resistor Colour Code Disc	£0.20
BP1	First Book of Transistor Equivalents and Substitutes	£1.50
BP2	Handbook of Radio, TV, Ind & Transmitting Tube & Valve Equivalents	£0.60
BP6	Engineers and Machinists Reference Tables	£0.75
BP7	Radio and Electronic Colour Codes and Data Chart	£0.40
BP14	Second Book of Transistor Equivalents & Substitutes	£1.75
BP24	52 Projects Using IC741	£1.75
BP27	Chart of Radio, Electronic, Semi-conductor and Logic Symbols	£0.50
BP28	Resistor Selection Handbook	£0.60
BP29	Major Solid State Audio Hi-Fi Construction Projects	£0.85
BP32	How to Build Your Own Metal and Treasure Locators	£1.95
BP33	Electronic Calculator Users Handbook	£1.50
BP34	Practical Repair and Renovation of Colour TVs	£1.95
BP36	50 Circuits Using Germanium, Silicon and Zener Diodes	£1.50
BP37	50 Projects Using Relays, SCR's and TRIACS	£1.95
BP39	50 (FET) Field Effect Transistor Projects	£1.75
BP42	50 Simple L.E.D. Circuits	£1.50
BP43	How to Make Walkie-Talkies	£1.95
BP44	IC 555 Projects	£1.95
BP45	Projects in Opto-Electronics	£1.95
BP47	Mobile Discotheque Handbook	£1.35
BP48	Electronic Projects for Beginners	£1.95
BP49	Popular Electronic Projects	£1.95
BP50	IC LM3900 Projects	£1.35
BP51	Electronic Music and Creative Tape Recording	£1.95
BP52	Long Distance Television Reception (TV-DX) for the Enthusiast	£1.95
BP53	Practical Electronics Calculations and Formulae	£2.95
BP54	Your Electronic Calculator and Your Money	£1.35
BP55	Radio Stations Guide	£1.75
BP56	Electronic Security Devices	£1.95
BP57	How to Build Your Own Solid State Oscilloscope	£1.95
BP58	50 Circuits Using 7400 Series IC's	£1.75
BP59	Second Book of CMOS IC Projects	£1.95
BP60	Practical Construction of Pre-amps, Tone Controls, Filters & Attenuators	£1.95
BP61	Beginners Guide To Digital Techniques	£0.95
BP62	Elements of Electronics – Book 1	£2.95
BP63	Elements of Electronics – Book 2	£2.25
BP64	Elements of Electronics – Book 3	£2.25
BP65	Single IC Projects	£1.50
BP66	Beginners Guide to Microprocessors and Computing	£1.95
BP67	Counter, Driver and Numeral Display Projects	£1.75
BP68	Choosing and Using Your Hi-Fi	£1.65
BP69	Electronic Games	£1.75
BP70	Transistor Radio Fault-Finding Chart	£0.50
BP71	Electronic Household Projects	£1.75
BP72	A Microprocessor Primer	£1.75
BP73	Remote Control Projects	£1.95
BP74	Electronic Music Projects	£1.75
BP75	Electronic Test Equipment Construction	£1.75
BP76	Power Supply Projects	£1.95
BP77	Elements of Electronics – Book 4	£2.95

BP78	Practical Computer Experiments	£1.75
BP79	Radio Control for Beginners	£1.75
BP80	Popular Electronic Circuits – Book 1	£1.95
BP81	Electronic Synthesiser Projects	£1.75
BP82	Electronic Projects Using Solar Cells	£1.95
BP83	VMOS Projects	£1.95
BP84	Digital IC Projects	£1.95
BP85	International Transistor Equivalents Guide	£2.95
BP86	An Introduction to BASIC Programming Techniques	£1.95
BP87	Simple L.E.D. Circuits – Book 2	£1.35
BP88	How to Use Op-Amps	£2.25
BP89	Elements of Electronics – Book 5	£2.95
BP90	Audio Projects	£1.95
BP91	An Introduction to Radio DXing	£1.95
BP92	Easy Electronics – Crystal Set Construction	£1.75
BP93	Electronic Timer Projects	£1.95
BP94	Electronic Projects for Cars and Boats	£1.95
BP95	Model Railway Projects	£1.95
BP96	C B Projects	£1.95
BP97	IC Projects for Beginners	£1.95
BP98	Popular Electronic Circuits – Book 2	£2.25
BP99	Mini-Matrix Board Projects	£1.95
BP100	An Introduction to Video	£1.95
BP101	How to Identify Unmarked IC's	£0.65
BP102	The 6809 Companion	£1.95
BP103	Multi-Circuit Board Projects	£1.95
BP104	Electronic Science Projects	£2.25
BP105	Aerial Projects	£1.95
BP106	Modern Op-Amp Projects	£1.95
BP107	30 Solderless Breadboard Projects – Book 1	£2.25
BP108	International Diode Equivalents Guide	£2.25
BP109	The Art of Programming the 1K ZX81	£1.95
BP110	How to Get Your Electronic Projects Working	£1.95
BP111	Elements of Electronics – Book 6	£3.50
BP112	A Z-80 Workshop Manual	£2.75
BP113	30 Solderless Breadboard Projects – Book 2	£2.25
BP114	The Art of Programming the 16K ZX81	£2.50
BP115	The Pre-Computer Book	£1.95
BP116	Electronic Toys Games & Puzzles	£2.25
BP117	Practical Electronic Building Blocks – Book 1	£1.95
BP118	Practical Electronic Building Blocks – Book 2	£1.95
BP119	The Art of Programming the ZX Spectrum	£2.50
BP120	Audio Amplifier Fault-Finding Chart	£0.65
BP121	How to Design and Make your Own P.C.B.s	£1.95
BP122	Audio Amplifier Construction	£2.25
BP123	A Practical Introduction to Microprocessors	£2.25
BP124	Easy Add-on Projects for Spectrum ZX81 & Ace	£2.75
BP125	25 Simple Amateur Band Aerials	£1.95
BP126	BASIC & PASCAL in Parallel	£1.50
BP127	How to Design Electronic Projects	£2.25
BP128	20 Programs for the ZX Spectrum & 16K ZX81	£1.95
BP129	An Introduction to Programming the ORIC-1	£1.95
BP130	Micro Interfacing Circuits – Book 1	£2.25
BP131	Micro Interfacing Circuits – Book 2	£2.25
BP132	25 Simple Shortwave Broadcast Band Aerials	£1.95
BP133	An Introduction to Programming the Dragon 32	£1.95
BP134	Easy Add-on Projects for Commodore 64 & Vic-20	£2.50
BP135	The Secrets of the Commodore 64	£2.50
BP136	25 Simple Indoor and Window Aerials	£1.95
BP137	BASIC & FORTRAN in Parallel	£1.95
BP138	BASIC & FORTH in Parallel	£1.95
BP139	An Introduction to Programming the BBC Model B Micro	£2.50
BP140	Digital IC Equivalents and Pin Connections	£3.95
BP141	Linear IC Equivalents and Pin Connections	£3.95
BP142	An Introduction to Programming the Acorn Electron	£1.95
BP143	An Introduction to Programming the Atari 600XL and 800XL	£2.50
BP144	Further Practical Electronics Calculations and Formulae	£3.75
BP145	25 Simple Tropical and M.W. Band Aerials	£1.95